~ Dedicated **t**o you – a **c**hil‹

FLAMES CAST NO SHADOWS

~-- ._.-~-._   .~.   _.-~-._.--~

First published in the United Kingdom in 2022 by The
Cloister House Press

ISBN 978-1-913460-58-7

<u>Index</u>

All chapters, arranged by the length of the poems:

Part one: The Spark (16 lines and less, pages 7 – 14)

Part two: The Fire (17 to 28 lines, pages 15 – 24)

Part three: The Blaze (29 to 48 lines, pages 25 - 43)

Part four: The Inferno (49 lines and more, pages 44 - 94)

All misery comes from privilege

And doubt, although a natural by-product of our
remarkable minds,

Is also the hardest aspect of being human.

There is a bright flame within us all –

A force of pure energy and no substance

And the brighter the flame, the darker the
shadows it casts.

If one can break through the mortal barriers
around their flame

And reach a doubtless state,

They have acquired one of the greatest
achievements available to an individual.

Where there is a light, there is always a shadow

And whatever cast it has at least two.

Though we may not see them (at least we don't now),

They have to go both ways – all of them do!

The tide can be low or the tide can be high

And if it is low, then the wind can be strong!

If there's no balance now, it will come with some time,

'Cause if it doesn't come, then it's all going wrong!

What comes up must come down – one-way tickets don't sell

And whoever knows that must have missed something else.

If you fall far below our societal norms,

You are raising the rest with one hand…in a sense.

So in short, live your life not regretting a thing

Because everything has universal resistance.

If you don't believe me, you're still not protected

From Maestra's eclectic and highly hypothetical theory of binary existence!

Part One: The Spark

QUESTIONS

They say: 'Question everything'.

All I question are answers.

There's more of them than questions

And questions cannot ask.

We ask into the void

Expecting to hear echoes,

Expecting us to grow.

Instead, we feel reduced.

A POET'S HEART

A poet's heart is full of hope,

Despite the daylight waning.

A poet finds a way to cope

In darkness and restraining.

An artist flies by means of sight

And meets themselves once more.

And only artists, only poets

Know what this is for.

REFLECTIVE SIGHT

When I was captured from behind

and deafened by the call of death,

I drowned it out, reached for my sharpness,

turned around and saw myself.

FRIENDSHIP

Life is a puzzle of boundaries unknown.

Its pieces are scattered through time and through space

And when you can't tackle its challenge alone,

You're helped by a kind and familiar face.

With friends, the daily is special indeed -

Their trust and their loyalty take you so far!

A friend will be there for as long as you need;

A true friend will be there as long as you are.

TRUE WEALTH

When endless days of toil subside

and worksheets don't pile by my side,

when deadlines don't become my lock

and I don't live inside a clock,

I'll work once more to reach new heights

with lavish riches in my sights.

Relentless as my budget soars,

until I step through gilded doors.

And then my wishes will run free,

but one demand remains in me:

I'll lie among the auburn leaves

in my majestic palace field,

too ready to give up my means

for my existence wealth to yield.

THE TEACHER

'It's quarter to nine: another lesson is to soon begin,

as is an opportunity for them to read all that is held therein,'

the teacher thought, and with a smile

glanced at the foreign names on the books in the pile.

'Here's Milton. But not the one from London.

And there is dark-skinned Einstein.

And this one teaches oriental history.

With these, I'll educate them in the world, not only in the classroom.'

A SONNET TO THE SONNET

We dug out speech from mass incongruence

And have exceeded our own language ever since.

Speech can't agree or argue, and it's sense

Is language's only method to convince.

And so the written word was carved unclear:

So promising of truth, but at what cost?

Sometimes it seems to be approaching near,

Until its bent trajectory is lost.

In writing sonnets, I stir the unknown.

I order silent letters, so they ring.

When read while not deemed purposeful, they groan.

When read in context with our life, they sing.

So here I make my little sonnet live -

Aside from words, I've nothing left to give.

Part Two: The Fire

[IS/ARE] [IS NOT] [AND]

Power is language

Language is not words

Mathematics is not numbers

Language and mathematics are shapes

Mathematics is language

Language is mathematics

Language and mathematics are storytelling

Storytelling is not verbal

Understanding is a series of well-placed connections

'Well-placed' is not intentional

Intention is unintentional

'Well-placed' is not unintentional either

A paradox is a paradox

Intention is pre-determined[error]

Intention is not pre-determined[error]

Power is eclectic

Eclectic power is wisdom

Wisdom is knowledge

Knowledge is not wisdom

Wisdom is storytelling

Storytelling is understanding and inspiration

Inspiration is love

Love is power.

ON THE NATURE OF NATURE

My thoughts are calm; their turbulence expelled.
Its reminiscence still rings in my ears.
Those feelings I feel that I've long reserved
For the season that ended all previous years.
The trees shed their colours all around me
As the wind dissipates all the strain in my mind,
And the clouds wash away with their drizzles of rain
All the pain and resentment this year left behind.

Like bare, crooked hands that wave me farewell,
The oak branches rustle their remaining leaves.
With each of my steps the howling breeze deepens,
Shooing the passer who already leaves.
I threw one last glance before quitting this park
Over decay and marshy footpaths:
All life and all beauty must face a decline,
But that wind is constant – no wonder it laughs.

And so I walk on after closing that gate,
Hoping this insight will close with its door.
A motionless victim to time's carousel,
I'll exit this cell, just to enter once more.

A CONVERSATION WITH MY REFLECTION

"So, Miss Maestra: it's time to take this work

outside your friendship circle – change the thinking of the world!"

"It's nothing short of controversial – are you stupid or insane?

All those times you'd tried to do it..."

"...all those times I'd tried in vain.

Well, nothing's final – let's start out small, alright?"

"No! Nothing's ever small enough

with crippling stage fright!"

"But if you shut up and let me try it out for once,

maybe I will cross the line..."

"...that pushed you back last time? No chance!"

"How about I smash that mirror

with a hammer, 'cause you suck!"

"You may just get away from me,

but not from seven years bad luck!"

"What? You're my reflection,

but you lie in all you say!"

"Cowards fear the naked truth -

if you're a coward, look away!"

"I'll look away to the beyond

and see there's nothing I could lose,

put on a show, and read my verse,

and leave them baffled and confused!"

"Read on, my kiddo: light their fires,

raise emotion in the air,

and be prepared for wild applause:

your strictest critic won't be there."

WHAT DO I OWE YOU, DARKNESS?

If all the world's a stage,

we cannot hide behind the scenes -

we're in the spotlight night and day.

Yet darkness lurks.

It's ever-present, even in the past and future.

Turn to it,

and it will hide

your guilt and pride.

When all those lights burn out

and heavy stage fog drowns our view,

I turn upstage and I drown, too.

I thank it, though

and feel its comfort.

It unmasks me of my role:

lets my thoughts

run free and deep

through high and steep.

What do I owe you, darkness,

for keeping all my deepest truths

within your spinning magnitude?

No light of day

will reach me now,

despite me being still exposed.

Let me spend

this moment here

that'll cost a year.

BY ORDER

The neighbours' child is out of doors again –
I think it's with that tree she spends the night.
Last week she asked her mother why it was
That grandpa's apple tree can't stand upright.

The rose bush that resides so near my home
Is neater than the truth it can express.
But when a group of youngsters gathered round,
One said: "It's so uneven! It's a mess!"

I saw a little boy get on the train
And all the way watch nothing but the moors.
And I was sure he didn't crave vast lands –
He wondered why the marsh looked wet and coarse.

And often do I hear this generation
Scrutinise imperfect blades of grass,
The lack of symmetry in chestnut leaves
And each unordered streak this planet has.

And often do I walk past glassy towers

While breathing in fumes from the motorway

And when the height of progress starts to dwarf me,

I'm only glad children are grown this way.

Nature has order that won't stand your ignorance

And keeping order is, I see, your duty.

Only when one surpasses the mundane

Does it begin to beckon with its beauty.

Part Three: The Blaze

WHEN THE CROWN WAS MINE

There was a day in my far past when I sat on the throne.

Nothing to do; nowhere to reach; nowhere to go.

The world cried when I dropped a single tear

And cheered up when I ordered so.

There I was worshipped, there was hailed and then again, alone.

On that same throne enclosed by wealth I spent each frozen day.

Nothing to want; nothing to think; nothing to say.

Somehow my stillness caused a jealous raid

Through which my country hacked as one,

United in their piety, as I sat locked away.

Away from violence, conflict and real, mortal demise;

Away from sacrificial acts and victors' cries,

I sat in mocking company of gold.

I sat and felt inanimate.

No one will know; no one will care; no one will sympathise.

I've always favoured the role of the funny jester

Or gallant deeds done by the knights of old.

But never have I thought that reign

Is not at all a fruitful game.

Illusive dreams disintegrate

The moment they come true - I knew

My royalty was social crime

Back when the crown, and all, was mine.

The last I heard were cracking walls and jangling painted glass,

As all my gold and velvet formed a ragged mass.

My fortress lay around me in collapse,

Before I noticed any change.

I lost hold of my country, so now I rule the world for once.

DON'T MIND ME, UNIVERSE

'Don't mind me', I exclaimed one night.

But no response, no presence glimmered in those porous heights.

The pondering that bore those words, and countless restless nights

Of sparking wisdom from my knowledge were in vain below those stars;

My brightest earthly ideations distantly diminished by their chars.

Each stately sphere has thus avenged me

Through my vacant eye, that smudged it into five sharp lines.

Or watched some feeble glow reflected in the lakes and brines,

Convinced that universal truth will serve me as a roofless church.

Some seek within; some seek without; and all are objects of another's search.

'Don't 'mind' me'. Is this what I said?

If only 'mind' can conjure up a presence in the vast,

Then what do 'heart' and 'soul' conceive? Or are they left for last

To act on what was so rehearsed and with such ease and flare performed,

And often to evade the justices that conscious moral thought has formed.

Don't mind me, little universe.

No, I do not discredit your unknown expanse for good -

I just accept your dominance over my flesh and blood

And how you've given me my reason; and like Tantalus himself

Have mocked me with it, watching me bundle your threshold further from myself.

Although, my boundless universe,

Now that I look at all your spangles through a mirror glass,

I see the very light you gave me so distinctly pass

Into a dozen orbits that light up for once my closed-up view.

And I begin to see my own reflection when I look above at you.

Don't mind me as I don't mind you.

There isn't much to mind when sight is always in my favour -

Not picking up the negative and choosing what to savour.

So what is all your endless shape if by it I can feel enclosed?

And what is your uncertainty if certainty is truly self-proposed?

One either drowns or one enlightens.

Perhaps from nearly drowning I've acquired this passive sense.

Truth has no language: someone, through a broken lens,

May see your stars as little crosses and pray for some divine splendour.

I will never know for certain.

So, Universe, to you I surrender.

THE DEN ON THE MOORS

I woke up in a feral thrill this morning,
Powered by the recall of your voice.
That radiation in your highest note
Called me to drive myself insane by choice.
Only in madness can I strive to understand
The limitless complexity of sound –
Perhaps I'll even speak to you illuded
By growing deaf to all the world around.

I stumble through the day in deepest awe –
You've opened up a portal into me
That will not seal until my dying day.
So many found themselves through you – they see
Deep-rooted wonder, locked by mundane life:
At different times and sites a different sight.
You occupy their scattered thoughts by day
And dominate devoted hearts by night.

I went out to your moors these past few days

And every time was led back to your house:

That grounded stony den could not reveal

A single flight endorphin you arouse.

I often wonder if you're ever there,

Maybe sat darkling, writing your next song.

Or maybe out to roam the windy moors.

Maybe one day you'll invite me along?

Your presence seems to end outside that screen

On which those millions go mad over your face.

When I explore this gloomy moor of yours,

I can't imagine fame in such a place.

You either have the courage to live quietly

Despite mountainous income in your bank

Or I've believed that you resided here

Because a pressman gave you such a rank.

Though day by day, I come back to your moor:

Sometimes to marching drumrolls of the storm,

Sometimes to howling pipes played by the wind.

Still, I've not seen a single human form.

If you did live here, I would see at least

A flicker of dim light within that den.

But something tells me you don't live elsewhere –

The pixel screen is where you live, and when.

32

MARY'S LITTLE LAMB

Mary had a little lamb

With white wool and white ears.

Where Mary ventures off to

Little Lamb always appears.

Mary's little lamb, though white,

Had a black spot on one horn.

Mary read it as an omen,

But that's just how lambs are born.

Mary went to school one day

So happy to see her friends,

But the class had finished soon

With Mary blamed for stealing pens.

Mary couldn't fathom why:

She won't steal! It's not fair!

But then Mary realised

Little Lamb wasn't there.

Mary once went to the mall

With the lamb by her side.

Just as she was exiting,

She was two trucks collide.

Soon the sirens called for her –
Oh, but why? It's not fair!
But then Mary realised
Little Lamb wasn't there.

Mary won't go out again.
Here she sits between four walls,
As she smells the burning wood
And the smoke alarm now calls.

Mary runs outside to find
Little Lamb, not at all white,
All in soot from horn to hoof
And with eyes gleaming bright.

Mary's lost her little lamb
Little lamb, little lamb,
Mary's lost her little lamb...

And I think we've found him.

THE LOST PHILOSOPHER

Death is twofold:

among the many ways in which life is,

death exposes the duality of thought;

letting the Mortals

and the Philosophers

take their final bows.

The ones that remain one with their corpse

since the second they die

are the certain, great Mortals –

each a different distance away from their counterparts

but equally imprinted on the historical map of the world.

The ones that lost themselves in life

and were found by others in death

are the everlasting Philosophers –

the beacons of their minds could outshine

any carnal flesh with ease,

and guide the generations

on their pilgrimage into themselves:

unveil to them the paradoxes that have always made sense;

the 'uni' in a unity; the 'one' that is in 'oneness';

the future on the outside

that's been the past inside us.

A good Philosopher is one who is lost.

A great Philosopher is never truly unhappy.

The Greeks have meaningfully crafted this title:

a 'lover of thinking' is a Philosopher –

one who embraces their primary mechanism

and manoeuvres their thoughts out of

every corner of unhappiness.

And a Mortal is every Philosopher.

As long as I hold life, life holds in me

the potential for both in death.

Whether a Mortal or a Philosopher in death,

a person thriving in life is in thought ever-uncertain

but at heart ever-decisive.

LONGING

We dream of a land far beyond the horizon
And we race to get there, no matter how long
It will take us to leave the explored and the used
To set sail for where we all deserve to belong.

We float with the wind as it plays in our sails,
The mild ocean breeze growing ever so strong.
But who are we to notice what pushes our boat?
All we need is the boat to push us along!

We're risking the trace of the dreams we've erased
To savour our lives in the brightest of colours.
The elements hinder us little by little,
Silently warning the lights try to lure us
With flattering promise of ending our longing:
That towers of prominence won't ever fall;
Our existance is feeding a power beyond us,
Igniting our purpose; warming us all.

Longing uprises when there's no way back.

As the waves start to climb and the night swiftly falls,

The ocean is raised by celestial force.

How could we lie above Nature's hand-woven laws?

It tosses our boat back and forth, like the rumours

That we've tossed around of the ultimate land.

Oh, we were so clueless of what we should crave

Over our homey bay and our motherly sand!

So let's set an anchor at where we were then -

Not all can afford to drift from the shore.

Wherever you are, there's a sea of desire

That's lying between all the rich and the poor

And the young and the old,

And the well and the ill.

The good and nirvana;

The bad and all hell.

This ocean's unstable, just like our yearnings

And settling down isn't what we do well.

FADED WALLS

Time does not fly:

Its pace cannot be measured.

Its reign is too sadistic;

Its weakness is its absence.

Until the hour rings

For cages to unhinge, the walls collapse

And puppets to tear up their strings,

There will be silence.

But can the silence speak?

We hear the news as drumming beats -

A rhythm lost in blind repeats, yet still

In every thump a life is lost

That shuts the doors of our retreats.

And now alone,

Enclosed in walls and hung on strings,

The puppeteers engraved on us what's truly gone.

Time's reign is too sadistic,

Even to our confinement.

Through faded walls

The rays may rip those strings

And spectral air may lift our souls,

But puppets can't stand up alone.

Control, a force of moderation, knows abuse -

When puppets can no longer read their masters' cues

Their lives are owned.

The faded walls forgotten.

And that's why we're still trapped here:

The cages shut; the strings torn off.

Their reign was too sadistic.

Their weakness was their absence.

BETWEEN FLOW AND STILLNESS

Along I float that splashing stream,
Along with my deep, daring dream
And with my shallow plan for when
I reach where I'll be swept to then.
Along I go with all the crowd:
Some humble and some ever proud,
Some behind and some before me,
And they all will hardly know me.

Those before me sometimes slowed
And were overtaken fast.
Some had deftly disappeared
Into the river cold and vast.
Only some had dissolved so,
But most continued in their flow
And the reason for this split
Is something I will never know.

Restlessly, we drift our routes,
All destined for the waterfall,
But all turning in different ways
At different times and different places
At our individual paces.

41

And here we pass a rock:

That rock had let our cold stream wrap it

For as long as it could stand.

It won't move and won't dissolve.

It won't shrink and won't expand.

Sure, there is no waterfall

For it to anxiously await –

Its presence has been fixed forever

By its placement's date.

You live outside of fear, old rock.

You've not escaped the flow, but still

Are shatterproof to every splash

And are indifferent to my will.

I cannot help but look in awe

And strive to grant myself this state.

Perhaps you, reading this, now know

That I've succeeded in this rate.

But why should people strive for stillness

When they were not born a rock,

And to find infinity

They suffer to outrun the clock?

Our chronal bodies are not cars

Which we at will command to park.

There's countless of us splashing through

And each have left the sand below their mark.

Between flow and stillness, there is life,

As much of which remains as what falls down.

Part Four: The Inferno

WISE FOOLERY

Sometimes it takes a lifetime to decipher blurred connections:

the kind that blends into itself – the kind that has reflections

in the undiscovered sections of some unrelated something.

Sometimes it takes a minute to perceive a blurred connection

and decipher what is in it.

But what line four is to line one is its reiteration –

sometimes the lifetime lasts a minute.

Such was the fate of one sly clown, so certain in his certainty

that shame, dishonour and defeat could not disrupt his narrative.

But would I call him sharp?

Oh yes, but even that's comparative.

His sharpness was on him and not within him, to be certain.

This blurred connection, in the end, had dropped the velvet curtain

over him, and only him.

Not long ago he stood right there, on that great stage of fools,

brought on to which all children cry, and that is no surprise;

particularly in the range of Clown himself, whom all despise.

One does not need to be a clown to be a fool, but still

a Fool can outwit any Clown without the need to kill,

as we shall see.

Among the many scornful stares that failed to reach his sense of shame

were eyes half-veiled by yellow curls; Fool was their owner's name.

At least to Clown it was, since he could scarcely see

past that blue cockscomb, that offbeat attire

and the burning jealousy that fool knew to inspire

with his unpolluted fame.

"Take off that hat!" Clown commanded, stepping closer to the fool.

"Those garish bells are just bizarre –

they do not fit the man you are!"

The fool locked glances with the rascal, but his face showed no surprise.

"You again, Clown - how could I stand here and fail to recognise

the coldest, slyest, greyest eyes?

I won't take off my hat, but I suggest you take off yours:

a frozen soul is something clown attire can't compromise."

Clown looked closely at the cockscomb sitting on Fool's yellow locks

and at its layer of protection outlined by metal blocks.

'It would not let through any blade,' he thought.

The fool saw his dismayed,

and asked: "you say I'm garish? Look at you, with three
contrasting colours running down that heavy cloak!

I still can't tell which one can't fit the other two in harmony.

If I were you, I'd choose with greater care the clothes that
armour me!"

To Clown's unseen surprise, he heard the ringing of the bells:

the bright blue cockscomb hanging now in his opponent's
hand,

his face and head were wrapped by hair the colour of warm
sand.

"Your wish came true, but what of it? It isn't raining now –

my hat won't serve my head as much as it would make it
bow."

Clown shook with rage: "all cowards play the brave by looking
so exposed,

but all that you've exposed to me are yellow coward's curls!

That straw should be tied into stacks and thrown inside the
farmer's car –

it does not fit the man you are!"

"And what change will suit your ideal? Would you rip the yellow out?

Then my vital courage will come through as red, without a doubt.

Touching my hair won't dirty you, but blood drowns in a single wave –

the stains won't wash away until the skin they're on has rotten in the grave.

You may believe that I have courage just as long as I can hold my head,

while all the red engulfs my yellow;

and the bravest I'll become is right before I drop down dead."

These words sounded clearer than speech. The scoundrel paused to think a while:

not once did Clown throughout his life perceive the nature of mortality.

That fool spoke strangely, and as if in sync with Clown's long dormant conscience.

He was so sharp, though seemed so dim - Clown loathed this odd duality.

With all the people on his side, the fool was held in many minds,

and none yet knew Clown had a sharpness that could end all other kinds.

"Off with those ugly shoulder plates! You can't afford to look a fool

when it's your wit that earned you status and became your sharpest tool!

You mustn't wear so much protection – my advice won't leave a scar.

It does not fit the man you are!"

Clown's tone sounded unwavering with all his doubts thrown back:

nothing uttered by this fool will stand a chance against attack.

He thought that his opponent will regardless look a foolish man,

if not through clothing, then through mockery, according to his plan.

But something striking skimmed across the fool's expression.

He stood immobile, his sight fixed on something in the distance,

though he retrieved inside himself - somewhere he often went.

His gaze now wild, he plainly knew the root of Clown's persistence.

"The combination of your words has spoken a whole different phrase -

one you yourself don't know, I'm sure.

That phrase described you with precision, and your three stripes reinforced it:

you've a plan, but I can see wise foolery has never crossed it.

Wit is a sharp tool, as you say, but sharpness cuts when in excess.

There is a sharper tool involved here - it's neither you nor me.

When I'm observing your three stripes, misconduct's all I see.

We all arose from even ground, yet only some to light progress.

We operate by one and two but adding three will mean 'regress'.

That off-tune chord, that mismatched colour left you cursed and never free.

Not only zebras get their stripes attracting shadows evenly.

You're doomed, you clown! Where there is evil, there is always three!"

Fool spoke these words with such a glint of malice in his sneer,

the poor old clown was handed chance

to see the ruins of his plans.

Alas, these ruins still deceived that Fool's demise was near.

There came a wave of silence, under which the clown was drowning.

It was as if Fool stole his voice and used it to double his own.

It was dishonour, not defeat to feeling which the clown was prone.

Hubristic sight can't pick up much, even the fact that Fool

without a question took the shoulder plates off too.

He dropped them down carelessly, deftly,

and his motion ended there.

For some time, the tortured two did not exchange a glare.

The clown still felt his pocket blade pricking him and prompting him.

He could not oppose the knife, or else this would not be the end

of all the scornful stares from people, all compulsions to pretend

to have the gift of endless courage, endless wit, and finite doubt

that will pull the nation to him and knock all his rivals out.

But Fool always knew what to say, and slicing the dense silence, spoke:

"the coldest, slyest, greyest eyes are not so grey as I now see.

How could I not have before seen that stream of green? Oh, silly me!

It's like an ivy-ridden pond colliding with an icy sea,

And tick by tock the ivy grows.

The next day all the brine will merge with ivy and the marshy pond,

and all its ice will melt away under your hot, passionate play.

Next week the ivy will mutate and mercilessly dominate

not just your eyes, but your whole face, externalising your disgrace.

And by next month no limb of yours will be saved by a thousand cures.

You won't be you, but untamed envy - be appalled! Be dazed! Ashamed be,

you green-eyed, three-striped monster..."

Fool looked down at the shoulder plates, continuing:

"You're quite a clown. It's fact. You're funny. Paradox, the root of humour,

serves you well. Shortly after ordering me to take off my 'garish bells',

you command the shoulder plates to come off too.

And strange this is – these shoulder plates are the most mundane

component of my outfit. Brown and basic. So different from the blue and yellow

scheme of my jacket. If anything, I would have expected the jacket to be criticised."

And with these words, Fool gathered up the remnants of the clown's design

to mock him down from his high rank and tossed it through the window.

The clown made foolish moves for sure, while Fool was clowning for a role.

The clown steered Fool but broke the wheel; now Fool drove the same brawl.

"Take off those loony pantaloons," Fool half-sang to himself.

"Something about them is bizarre –

they do not fit the man you are!"

"You half-breed! What do you allow yourself?" The clown screeched, as if feral.

"Oh really, ratbag? I thought you were hardened to all things explicit!

I know they're 'garish', as you say; so take your peevish, greenish eyes

off where they are and point them someplace where there's nothing they could mar -

they do not fit the boy you are!

Throw off those shoes while you're at it – what are those inward-curling flaps?

If one unties, you'll trip over and fall so very far –

it would not fit the man you are!"

Sharply, Fool flung his jangling cockscomb at the rascal's foot.

The clown reacted fast, yanked up his leg, and felt a cut.

The third stripe glowed its mismatched colour.

The off-tune chord had rung; and snapped a second later.

The ivy-ridden, icy pond that once resided in his eye

was seeping through his punctured thigh.

It crawled out, hardly red.

Whatever bile was mixed in with his blood

looked just as vile as the imposter's every word.

The many coins in the clown's pocket clashed with the precision of that blade.

The knife played them like organ keys,

as if to mourn the sinner it's betrayed.

The coins soon started slipping out of the mangled pocket

and splashed into the pool of blood in which the clown now kneeled.

That fool stood where he always stood, collected as he ever was.

"You came onstage with little sale and drift out with these meagre earnings.

No true riches can be claimed after such a grim defeat.

I'm as certain as can be that these few coins will not repay

the lives you took, nor your own life, nor the control you've craved each day.

The velvet curtain falls as fast as the imposter's rise to fame:

once the imposter's mask is snatched, he dies. Oh, what a shame!

So tell me, Clown:

why is it, fool,

that though my armour was addressed

as dim-witted and taken off,

it's you who lies undressed?"

TIME VESSEL

You are a time vessel –

A titanium ship,

Weightlessly navigating the infinite quantum

Of void and substance.

You are an atom –

A beyond-microscopic force,

Supporting and being supported by billions of its kind,

No two of which are the same in complimenting this Earth.

You co-exist in favour of each other,

Reacting with oddities without which there will be no 'be'

To form the impact written in its entirety

In the prints of the great algorithm.

With every tik of the omnipotent hand of the classroom clock,

A thought slides over another in a desperate attempt

To stop it – to overpower the greatest force.

The teacher carries on teaching;

The distant sirens carry on howling;

The girl next to me drops her pen for the twelfth time.

I seem to be alone in my quest.

I came onto this arena knowing I had already lost,

Simply by having such a mission.

The passing of time should not be felt, else something is wrong;

And all my classmates seem to have it right.

What use is there in sinking into

The most unforgiving of dimensions,

And letting my undying, unfulfillable longing for life devour me

While the rest of the world lives in harmony

With the clocks they had never provoked?

Suddenly, time has awakened me from time:

That classroom clock has screeched its deadly cry

And swept the children onto the playground

Within seconds...no, half a second. Or a millisecond? No...

Again, I witnessed the fearless conquest of the wooden tower.

Again, the climbing frame was engulfed by boys and girls

Of all ages, of all positions on the fourth dimension –

Our collective antagonist whom they haven't yet met.

They simply don't know; they haven't learnt.

They haven't lost; they haven't gained.

Their unconditional excitement ebbs and flows

And their relationship with time had little progress.

I observed that relationship

Even in their positions on that climbing frame:

The oldest boy sat the highest;

The smallest girl laboriously clambered onto the preceding step.

Here it was: the priority line of life.

Time lifts us higher, and higher,

Our view of the land below expanding with each year,

As we float higher and higher,

And right into the heavens.

'Right' into the heavens... never left.

The clocks must only go right for a reason.

Yes, right! The clocks were always right!

Their inventors were right,

And the inventor of all inventors was right!

This is how it was intended – it is right for time to pass

And it's right for us to fear the power over us it has!

Without time, there'll be no 'time' and no such questions to discuss -

We were products of the clock before the clock was made by us.

I wouldn't be surprised if even Planet Earth spins right,

Or if the limits of the world are not the limits of my sight.

The fourth dimension is a tool through which we comprehend

The foundations of a force that makes us think we'll face an end

But never lets us know we're dead – I see,

Life has no end for me.

This knowledge is calming.

It must be right too.

I shouldn't spend my time on time.

I should live my life as a jigsaw piece

To this strange universe

And bond with my earthly companions

Over the similarities all of our differences leave us with.

Through this life, we see beauty that can never be ultimately described

Further than with the word 'right'.

We were born free, yet in time's tightening chains,

And through accepting inferiority we become powerful.

That's quite funny...as is life.

It's just an elaborate joke that takes a while to get,

And the laughter at the end is worth it all.

And there I hear the call of the clock, somehow mellower and quieter than before.

The climbing frames are vacant now and the swings still in recoil.

It's only been ten minutes,

But they have grown me more than the past week could.

The time vessel is taking a turn:

It evolves itself through an external prompt.

That unforgiving dimension does to each vessel

What has never been done before

To any particle it bore.

I must be its chosen.

It has expired my ignorance.

Thank you, time.

VISUAL SOUND

If there's a colour spectrum and a rainbow of laws
Which our eyes abide and train us to ignore its flaws,
Then what is sound, if it isn't waves that pass through air?
Invisible geometry we don't suspect is there?

You may not want to know, if music colours in your day.
'If music be the food of love, play on', is what they say.
The melody is sacred, but is never out of reach -
A maxim the composer and the listener both teach.

And here I am,
Beneath the gradients of altered shades the falling sun has left
behind.
The sky seemed to get darker, but the colours only thrived!
Like poppies on a battlefield, released by fading light,
They decorate its passing; then welcome in the night.

I stood there, marvelled.
Not only could I see this sight, but I could hear it too:
The gentle prelude, then a grand surprise,
All counterplayed by sadness that I see behind my eyes.

The sun has left the sky by now.

Left me, with all my fantasies of beauty

Frozen; thinking.

'It's my duty to express this,' I thought,

Almost aloud.

I set off to get home before it gets too dark and late,

But all the way

The voice of doubt

Screamed of

This concept's fate.

How was I meant to capture this?

It black on white?

In notes?

Condense it into symbols

And explain what it denotes?

I'm entering my home;

Not switching on the lights.

I want the darkness to propose how I spend most my nights.

I'm walking over to my instrument

Before the giant window,

And I close my eyes.

'Visual sound? How juxtaposed! The two cannot amount!

You're not supposed to hear a sight!

You just can't see a sound!'

You might be right; I'm likely wrong –

On me this has no hold.

It only matters that you're right if others are involved.

But who is there to see me play with tunes, all in my head?

Or draw them into diagrams, or painting them instead?

It's stunning what the black and white piano can express,

The black and white sheet music, and the black orchestral dress!

To others, I create. I do it for myself, of course.

They can't, however, see the wavelengths in my eye

As I absorb the rhythms all around me, whether I

Am in a cinema, a theatre or passing by a club.

Sometimes I hear the sunset; sometimes I see the music – the cycle never ends.

I'm blessed with every moment, but I can't share it with friends.

So far, it's been a solo game with just a single view.

I'm not a glitch – there must be others!

Could it be you?

KING REGARDS, YOUR YOUNGER SELF

Dear M,

I love you.

That's not easy to say,

or else I won't be writing rhymes, hoping you would forgive my crimes.

Love may be chaos in disguise, but chaos can't be true to hate.

Nothing's more complex than learnt methods masquerading as innate.

You've learnt to hate me when you left me: stuck in time; stuck within you

and if I didn't make you hate me, you won't love the present you.

Though in my day, I loved the world:

unconditionally, freely.

I've figured out that innate hate

never could be felt sincerely.

You're scared of me; I'm not of you –

how can you fear your younger self?

Yes, you can hate me all you want –

I tore your self-respect, your health,

your unconditional approval of conditionally good

events, and sights, and many people whom you'd hardly understood.

All this is quite a cause for hate, but hate is not a cause for
fear.

Hate is too bright; fear is too dark, where light of hate does not
come near.

It seems that hate possesses fear, but fear cannot experience
hate.

Fear can't feel love, but hatred can - between them, is there
love or hate?

And once you're blinded by your hate and light can't reach you
from above,

the world looks calm, nothing like fear – welcome to the world
of love!

You stand upon a bridge of knowledge, crossing wailing waves
of time,

but I am far below that bridge. I see your face, and you see
mine.

I don't know you, so cannot cross; and you may judge me from
above,

but know: though they are small and far, your memoires are
all you are.

You threw me down beneath the waves -

a little sacrifice to time,

which also paid you back with luck,

a lantern to light up fear's mine,

a cover for the blinding hate,

and love for love – the purest kind!

I thank you for my early fate

and love you, more than hate could hate.

Of course, that's not my verse you've read –

it came entirely from your head

and from your memory of me:

I've made you all you've longed to be!

THERE'S NOTHING QUITE LIKE A FRESH SUMMER STORM

There's nothing quite like a fresh summer storm:

Tumultuous gales sweeping fast through the leaves,

Sweeping through the blue hues of the still-heated sky

And collecting a rustling choir of the flora nearby.

There's nothing quite like a warm summer rain

Shaking rust from the clouds; waking them from their sleep

And erasing the dust from the dry, rocky paves

Of the sea-smothered cliffs and the battered and half-open caves.

Through the hum of the breeze, quiet chatter is heard:

Faces peering through windows of rain-sheltered cafes,

Watching the raindrops unite with the sea

As if sunny siestas and long, cloudless days are a sight that they won't again see.

There's nothing quite like an outburst of thunder

Through limitless fields of yellowing grass,

And there's nothing like wilting and bent-over trees

Animated with dew; shining like giant emeralds, drinking the streams the storm frees.

Now the sailors have pulled covers over their boats

And the farmers have enclosed their livestock in barns.

Talk of short, shallow rivers spilling into a flood

And of imminent changes in climate released out to roam
through the damp and devoid neighbourhood.

There's nothing quite like suspense greater than its trite
cause...

Who knew that these past days of crowds on the beach,

Choking heatwaves and blinding, incandescent light

That made people go wild: made them dance, made them
scream,

Hold to one like a trance; fade away like a dark, drunken
dream?

I watched those that I thought have known this too soon:

Little feet patting through the wet, curdling sand;

Little hands tearing off covers from creaking boats;

Little sparkles of giggles within little cots.

Children flew through the storm with its vigour embraced.

Others played in the boats; others hid, sought and chased,

And the lock of the hen coop was tossed to the ground

As the youngest of them trailed the hens all around.

They respond to the thunder; they pity the clouds

That have clashed once again and are shedding their tears.

They believe winds can cry about their child-like fears.

They can't see that such storms cloud their fantasies in future years.

And a part of me will always dance through the storm,

Though they don't always rumble through Edenic summers.

And childhood is endless – a freedom-filled cage

That expands with experience, never collapsing with age.

Yes, there's nothing quite like a fresh summer storm:

There's nothing quite like the rainbow it leaves.

THE TREE OF LIFE

Clear, uncommonly blue skies
Hover over leathered leaves.
Fresh, uncommonly green grass
Nestles in earth's sturdy weaves.
And among it stands the Tree,
As she stood a thousand years.
Fed by rich, dishonoured bodies,
Watered by pure, enslaved tears.

Art and knowledge grew her tall;
Death and woe had grown her strong.
Every leaf contains a right;
Every bark contains a wrong.
And the wisp of cloudy haze,
If it ever passed her by,
Dances round her like a halo
While inviting her to fly.

This is how it was.

But only weeks ago a neighbour tree had fallen.

She lay half-sunk into the grass, half-raised by rocks that caught her.

The remnant of her smooth, young stem had split the forest into two,

With slanted trees on either side, as if in fear of what had brought her

Down.

And so a piece of bronzy bark had chipped too, from the Tree of Life.

An ancient piece – perhaps one that had seen the fall of man.

The Tree still felt the axe's blow and golden sap has filled her wound

And blanketed the fallen piece: if man can fall, then bark too, can.

If man can fall, he can avenge the tree he deemed responsible

And let his own persuaded flaw roam innocent and free.

Then man himself will be avenged by it and fall again,

And we all know in what place our next landing will be.

This is how it was.

But just one week ago the hunter came and shot a doe.

His bullet long had lost its echo, while the doe's cry hadn't ceased,

And still it lingers in the mist that veiled that forest ever since.

Birds weren't singing – they were silent, thinking what brought the deceased

Down.

And so the Tree of Life had trembled, trembled until one bright leaf

Was severed at the very stem and glided down, down underneath.

And by the time it touched the grass, it hardly looked like any leaf –

All brown and rotten, it split up and was enveloped by the heath.

And then another leathered leaf was severed by uncharted force.

It too had flown away, decaying; followed by one green leaf more.

Soon, the Tree of Life will die if man's will won't change its course.

For each death, a leaf is lost; thus, the doe's bloodline was mourned.

This is how it was.

Though just three days ago a thousand fish washed up on shore:

Some tangled up in plastic sheets; some still exhaling their last breath.

Some had lost their life in struggle; some had many lives inside them

Which were never granted chance before man sent polluted death

Down.

After he sent polluted death, no conscience spoke to man – instead,

He stormed onto the shore before collapsing on a murky wave.

And there he splashed, and there he thought himself to dominate the water,

With no gills and with no flippers; drownable; the ocean's slave.

Only the Tree of Life knew truth: that was man's disregard for woman –

Mother nature, the first bearer, did not sin in making sinners,

Whilst the sinners sinned against themselves and their own future lives.

Without trees and without wildlife, they won't live to think they're winners.

All the while the ancient Tree was weeping tears of saltless brine

From every crevice of her trunk and from her deep, majestic roots

Far underground, as if to donate any remnants to the oceans

And to purify in vain mankind from all the life it loots.

This is how it was.

But only yesterday the last of icebergs had dissolved.

It melted into icy foam from underneath the little bear,

Whose childish cry out to her mother had dissolved, just like the ice.

And so she sank, out of this world, out of her mother's tender care

Down.

The end was coming near for all, as it was near for the Great Tree.

The cloudy haze that rarely came now draped her branches all around

In white burial drapery, to help man's victim be set free

From all her children wronged her of.

Farewell, champions...

This is how it is.

Today, that Tree is not of Life,

With her trunk now fuelling fires

And her leaves nowhere in sight

Since the doe's life had been taken.

Her bark screeched as it caught fire,

Not for human ears to hear –

They only felt the heavy air

And struggling for breath, they watered her.

This didn't solve their troubles, though. Indeed, the air was running out,

As was clean water

And all produce

And materials.

Still ignorant; still petulant is man.

He does not feel – he only thinks,

Or so he thinks.

Man sold his life to his own mother

Without thought and without feeling,

In the name of pushing progress to the brinks:

Up.

This is how it is.

And just right now, one has collapsed.

Soon, man will fall again.

PENDULUM

As the stars raised their glow and the sun travelled down,
My dirt road began passing through a small town.
A peculiar place – no built lights were in sight;
Little huts with straw roofs almost drowned in the night.
Enclosed by a fence of coldly steep hills,
There were charts on the walls, demonstrations of skills,
Plans of many recalled generations
Who lived, laughed and left behind their creations.

My path carried on, but I strayed away
To a barn full of sheep and a hut full of hay.
Somewhere distant, I barely made out guitars ringing
And echoes of voices, merrily singing.

Though the spring air is always colder up high,
Not a tickle of wind could be felt passing by.
I was shielded by hills and illusions of warmth
From a far-glowing fire, like the star of the North.
It was centred between a small hut and a field,
Likely used for the yield
Of a crop of some sort.

The nibbling of the cold quickly warped into deep bites of frost,

And I turned to the flame, setting off for the heat;

Feet numb.

The nearer I drew, the brighter it beamed;

The brighter it beamed, the faster it danced;

And the faster it danced, the sharper my sense of a newfound sight:

I've seen heaters on poles and grey clouds over chimneys,

But felt just the warmth in a room with a roof.

Yet this fire showed protection; rising low, then high

As smoke strands that fly to the half-darkened sky.

Settling down near the blazing wood, I looked over to the field.

Not much but dim rows of dirt and a dark form could be revealed.

The form took a step, feeling my stare; 'squeal' went the gate;

And suddenly, an elder man's shadowed stare

Broke through the orange flare.

I couldn't speak a word, but my eyes fixed on his; not by choice.

Having read my alert, he sat opposite me; hood pulled down.

No, he wasn't wary of intruders, nor had malice planned –

He wept.

I wanted to say…something.

What brought him to tears?

I should at least ask.

What language did he speak?

Was I the reason?

"Excuse me," I whispered.

He looked up at me.

"You see," he began, not awaiting my question,

"April takes its last breaths while May spreads its wings,

But my rye hasn't sprouted, nor has it died.

It's between all the layers,

Still deep inside.

This isn't my first confrontation with chance –

This has happened before.

They neither die, nor do they live –

They just don't grow.

The seeds are not dead – their potential is full

But the earth drowned them whole.

There are always two outcomes, and that leaves a space

For a 'no'.

Life's a duel. Like this rye,

We won't win; we can't die.

We just fight, and fight on

Against time, on our own."

His English was impeccable: no dialect was to be heard.

In fact, he sounded quite like me – the English that I'd learnt.

And what a way with words he had…what thoughts lived in his head!

While spending days at work in fields,

Or making charts, or milking cows,

He noticed it all in the brightest of lights:

Noticed the rye was just stuck, not dead.

By then, all traces of the sun had condensed into white stars,

And the fire seemed taller and brighter than it was before.

Not a single log was thrown in, but still it grew;

Still in control.

The man stood up, gestured at me to follow him, and up got I.

We passed some wells and cattle sheds before we reached his home.

He had not electricity, no TV and no phone.

His house was made of ancient logs and held with dirt and clay.

He had a cosy bed of straw and for a pillow, hay.

I saw a freshly cut tree trunk that served me as a chair,

So I sat down and heard him sigh, cleaning of straw his hair.

"We're standing on a pendulum; life operates the swing," he said.

"Its every shift scatters all chance – the door to everything.

One day, you'll rise so high the only way left will be down,

And past the down point up you go, until again you're facing down.

But there's one moment so, so brief, to many it's invisible.

The lowest point – ninety degrees – where potential is divisible.

Life rocked my swing so hard it nearly flipped it on its side,

But then I took control, found balance, and enjoyed the ride.

People are like my rye crops: they haven't died but haven't lived,

Although perhaps they're doing both.

The lowest point is underground –

From there, it's only growth."

Having spoken, the man shuffled into his bed of straw

And turned on his side.

Through a half-shattered window, I saw the townspeople

Dancing, playing, singing,

As if unaware of the failed crops.

And the small, burning pit had already flourished into a giant bonfire,

With children standing around it and indulging in its warmth.

Their incredible hopefulness,

The complete absence of wind in the area

And their timeless culture

Conveyed a sublime sense of eternity –

It felt surreal.

Their philosophy was not corrupted by unneeded knowledge.

Hence, there was no room for doubt.

To this day, I am in awe of the old man

Who had directed his grief at forever altering my perspective.

All our lies reflect truth.

All our lives serve as proof.

Without rain, nothing grows.

Without pain, nothing flows.

UNITITLED

'I left this world five days ago.

I don't remember where I went,

but nothing seems in its right place:

the moon has fallen, foxes scream

and nobody is seen outside.

Where did they all go?

What has happened to my distant, although just-abandoned life?

Am I in it now?

Then how do I know I'm alive?

There's only one way to go: ok, I'll look inside myself.

Don't worry, all I'm doing is beginning to regress

back to where I was enclosed and re-enter all this mess...

I saw myself, as if through a telescope –

all earthly chains unbound,

walking with endless eagerness under the sun

and casting no shadow...

Oh,

but I don't think I've left.

Perhaps it was a dream – oh yes,

a simple piece of neural footage

that resembled all the mess

I now recall.

So don't you fret – I know I'm sleeping

and you've joined me for a night

just to sit and ask me questions,

maybe dabbling in my fright.

My own brain must be asking me

why I assign my dreams such value.

ante liberans te, libere alium.

So where was I?

Ah, yes. The changes.

Mostly visible by day.

And the nights must be the same.

But again, it's May –

of course the nights are warm as days...

by the by, it's been five days since I left this world...I mean,
the waking one.

Did I tell you this?

Why? What have I done wrong this time?

Have you ever thought that this

is why people leave this world?

Because of individuals

who criticise their every word!

If you could prove to me you're qualified enough

to ask me twenty questions in a way that's though

to answer, I will pay you more

than anyone who could have chosen

to employ you would have paid.

Alright, I'll stop provoking you, no matter who it is you are.

I'm better off keeping you on my side, just in the case

of that strange world returning...or my own return to it.

If that shall happen, I'll need twenty more questions asked
face to face.

But anyway, you wanted more of that strange tale: I digress

and back into where I have been these past few days – this
mindless mess...

I've left this world four days ago to visit my site of anagnorisis.

Ah, here they are: the crimson trees dripping with blood.

How beautiful a sight – how rare and how insightful...

I've never before thought a person was just like a tree –

with complex networks of blue veins filled up with hot, red blood;

with storage leaves, just like the cells that make up you and me.

These trees' own inner lives are stored in every cell of that blue wood,

and there they make their sorrows bleed

whilst pulling them out of their world.

That's how they've stood for these four years:

one sorrow less, one bright day more;

and every drop of blood will water them

to help them grow.

They grow from their sorrows...

and so did I, that disinhibited stray loon

that walked under the scorching sun,

under the nitrogenic moon,

and cast no shadow.

No substance will stand in the way

of my incandescence – the day

of every dawn and dusk had lived inside me all along

to cast a shadow on each block that lies below my flaming node,

and shroud the grounded ones in darkness – just where they belong.

This place was full of the deserving:

the only crowd that honoured sorrow –

the sole seer of oppression in a person's only self:

their memories.

It's what I hate to recall now

that has endowed me with that flame.

To others, it's a gift of light;

to me, it's the seal of my name

on everything I come to touch

and char with long-suppressed black wrath.

Even the whitest, purest substance

cannot stray from my dark path.

Hydrogen does not diminish,

oxygen does not make rise

the anomalous thermology

of my wrath's hard-earned prize.

I water it with sacred blood

gathered from my crimson trees,

but it won't need blue wood to burn:

instead, it burns through me.

You're giving me the silent treatment now?

Is this the 'treatment' you've disclosed in your report?

No...you...you can't...

I'm not crazy! I swear on my abnormal sanity!

I saw what I saw, and if you're truly in my brain,

you should have access to these memories to prove I'm not insane!

I'm right until I'm proven wrong.

And if I state in clear coherence that I haven't been away,

and that everything I've told you had comprised one crazy day

on this planet and this earth, will you stop in what you say?

You cannot deem me crazy if I don't feel harmed by unique thoughts.

Your deeming doesn't stand a chance against God's pre-drawn lots.

I left this world three days ago, and just to make it clear for you,

I hadn't left this planet since the day I came out of the womb.

To some degree, I think you're right:

it isn't common to experience

betrayal by your sight.

But now at least, I see.

I see, you question me.

So let me question you as well:
would you believe that I had doubts
of my transient whereabouts,
and that resulted in this mess
to which I constantly regress?

I don't remember any harm
or violent state of alarm
enforced on me in that red wood
with blue trunks draped in crimson blood.

Alright, I hear you too have doubts
of my transient whereabouts.
But leaving this world for a day
is what we do sometimes. Ok?
You cannot tell me that you're not
unhappy sometimes with the lot
that planet earth offers to you
and wish to alternate the view
from time to time!

But then I know I've had the need

for glory and strength on repeat.

I'm lost in visions of a place

where I exist in any case.

It's all I ever knew to need,

and need is all I ever knew.

But who alive won't need to know if they

were born to need, or to the few who threw their needs away?

Who threw their needs away?

Yes.

What's so intriguing about that?

I don't remember who had raised me,

nor do I exactly care.

It won't matter in my life

which is...by no means fair.

But it will matter, won't it?

It already does?

Well, it shouldn't.

I left this world two days ago

and I still feel that ruthless rain

drowning me in all my pain...

the rain must be what made the blood

so swiftly drip down the blue wood...

I know what I have seen, perhaps clearer than the life

I see each day – the life that's veiled by strife.

I don't know if the rain was what

made all these crimson trees grow tall -

I thought it did at first, but now

I recall that it drowned them all.

The ones that didn't grow so tall

by not drinking the blood of sorrow

did not live to see tomorrow.

It drowned me too –

drowned me in recollection:

drowned me in me,

if memories are all I am.

So I must be...be my own death?

What happened to incandescence?
All I recall are shadows now.

There must have been another source
far higher and broader in course
than that illusion I believed
to think I shone, and be relieved.
That source had blinded me at first
and then exposed me to myself:
the shadowed, undistinguished mess
to which I despise to regress.
And that just proves my point once more:
this world has closed on me its door.

I cannot bear to think of trouble.
My resistance has run out.
It was washed off by the rain
and blown out by shadowed doubt.
What is there now left for me?
To exist, and nothing more?
Tell me, how can I escape?
How do I live? I implore!

I'm all alone, away from light.
A mere schoolgirl,
left even by childish fright.

But shadows and reflections are proof that something exists,
you say?

How can that be?

Yes, I do agree.

I only know I live by instinct – not by thought.

I think enough to know I don't.

You know what? You're right.

Oh, yes you are!

All that I see is in the scope

of my incessant strive for hope!

I cannot look outside my vision

or imagine a new colour,

just as I can't stray away

from my guide – happiness!

Though casting shadows with my mortal form,

I can return to pure expression, and inform

that same real world that it was wronged,

and that's why it now knows to wrong itself!

I left this world one day ago.

Crimson trees; incessant rain.

They were not what brought me pain…

Though the shorter trees were drowned,

All the taller have collapsed.

They can't grow up anymore

After a certain height is passed.

Life's not an endless strive for height,

although emotion is indeed.

Uncertainly is interest.   Interest is certainty.

   It is not about   how I' m seen at

arrival.   It's about how I'm   seen at departure.

    Death is   the next best thing

after   life.

Then   is it   right   to write?

    Most writers   are

wrongers,   but they write left to right.

I saw distorted   visions in the   joy-driven scope   of

    my   head.

              I left this   world,

   so now   I write my own,'

       I once said.

CPSIA information can be obtained
at www.ICGtesting.com
Printed in the USA
LVHW021506310822
727116LV00004B/191